Homemade Hand Sanitizers, Face Masks, Sanitizing Wipes.

How to Make Safety Face Masks and Hand Sanitizers at Home.

Text Copyright [Sara Blakely]

All rights reserved. No part of this guide may be reproduced in any form without permission in writing from the publisher except in the case of brief quotations embodied in critical articles or reviews.

Table of Contents

Homemade Hand Sanitizers,...................1
Face Masks, Sanitizing Wipes..................1
How to Make Safety Face Masks and Hand Sanitizers at Home........................1
Table of Contents......................................3
Introduction..9
Chapter 1 Face Masks............................14
Chapter 2 Different Types of Face masks and Who Needs them During the Coronavirus Pandemic...........................16
Chapter 3 Make Face Masks at Home....18
    Safety Face Mask Recipe № 1..........................18
    Safety Face Mask Recipe № 2..........................19
    Reversible and Washable Face Mask Recipe №3 20
    Homemade DIY N95 Type Face Mask Recipe №4 21
    Medical Mask at Home....................................23
Chapter 4 WHO and CDC Hand Washing Recommendations...............................29
Chapter 5 Homemade Hand Sanitizer Recipes...32
    Basic Hand Sanitizer Recipe............................32
    Aloe Vera Hand Sanitizer.................................32
    Rose Hand Sanitizer...33
    Chamomile Hand Sanitizer..............................34

Aloe Vera, and Tea Tree Hand Sanitizer...........34
Lemon and Lavender Hand Sanitizer...............35
Basic Hand Sanitizer Recipe............................36
Aloe Vera and Grapefruit Hand Sanitizer.........37
Soothing Lavender Hand Sanitizer...................37
Aloe Vera and Lavender Hand Sanitizer...........38
Tea Tree Hand Sanitizer...................................38
Aloe and Tea Tree Hand Sanitizer....................39
Clove and Lavender Hand Sanitizer.................40
Vitamin E and Tea Tree Oil Hand Sanitizer......40
Aloe and Eucalyptus Hand Sanitizer................41
Aloe Vera Hand Sanitizer.................................42
Roman Chamomile and Aloe Vera Hand Sanitizer 42
Basic Hand Sanitizer..43
Hand Sanitizer Recipe......................................43
Vinegar Disinfectant..44
Lavender Disinfectant......................................44
Cinnamon and Tea Tree Hand Sanitizer...........45
Oregano and Aloe Hand Sanitizer....................46
Tea Tree and Eucalyptus Hand Sanitizer..........47
Lemon Essential Oil Gel...................................47
Aloe Vera Gel Disinfectant...............................48
Myrtle and Aloe Essential Oil Gel.....................49
Carrageenan Hand Sanitizer............................49
Carrageenan and Sandal Hand Sanitizer..........50
Simple Disinfectant Recipe..............................51
Vitamin E and Rosemary Disinfectant Recipe...52

- Tea Tree Oil Disinfectant Recipe.......................52
- Orange and Aloe Vera Disinfector....................53
- Orange and Lemon Hand Disinfector..............54
- Lavender Oil Disinfectant..................................54
- Vitamin E and Tea Tree Oil Disinfectant Recipe 55
- Coconut Oil Hand Disinfector..........................56
- Thyme and Aloe Disinfectant...........................56
- Clove and Tea Tree Oil Disinfectant................57
- Cinnamon, Eucalyptus Hand Disinfector..........57
- Cinnamon Disinfectant Spray...........................58
- Oregano and Aloe Disinfectant.........................59
- Tea Tree Oil Hand Disinfector..........................60
- Four Ingredients Hand Sanitizer......................60
- Batch Hand Sanitizer..61
- Four Ingredient Hand Sanitizer II....................63
- Original Hand Sanitizer....................................63
- Hand Sanitizer with Vitamin E........................64
- DIY Hand Sanitizer...65
- Liquid Soap...66

Chapter 6 Sanitizer Wipes.......................68
- Homemade Sanitizer Wipes.............................68
- Antibacterial Wipes..69
- Sanitizer Wipes №1..70
- Sanitizer Wipes №2..73
- Sterilizer Wipes..74

Conclusion..77

Introduction..6

Chapter 1 Face Masks..........................10

Chapter 2 Different Types of Face masks and Who Needs them During the Coronavirus Pandemic..........................12

Chapter 3 Make Face Masks at Home....14

    Safety Face Mask Recipe № 1..........................14

    Safety Face Mask Recipe № 2..........................15

    Reversible and Washable Face Mask Recipe №3 16

    Homemade DIY N95 Type Face Mask Recipe №4 17

    Medical Mask at Home..................................18

Chapter 4 WHO and CDC Hand Washing Recommendations..................................23

Chapter 5 Homemade Hand Sanitizer Recipes..26

    Basic Hand Sanitizer Recipe...........................26

    Aloe Vera Hand Sanitizer...............................26

    Rose Hand Sanitizer......................................27

    Chamomile Hand Sanitizer.............................28

    Aloe Vera, and Tea Tree Hand Sanitizer..........28

    Lemon and Lavender Hand Sanitizer...............29

    Basic Hand Sanitizer Recipe...........................30

    Aloe Vera and Grapefruit Hand Sanitizer.........30

    Soothing Lavender Hand Sanitizer..................31

    Aloe Vera and Lavender Hand Sanitizer..........31

    Tea Tree Hand Sanitizer................................32

Aloe and Tea Tree Hand Sanitizer..................32
Clove and Lavender Hand Sanitizer................33
Vitamin E and Tea Tree Oil Hand Sanitizer......34
Aloe and Eucalyptus Hand Sanitizer...............34
Aloe Vera Hand Sanitizer................................35
Roman Chamomile and Aloe Vera Hand Sanitizer 35
Basic Hand Sanitizer......................................36
Hand Sanitizer Recipe....................................36
Vinegar Disinfectant.......................................37
Lavender Disinfectant....................................37
Cinnamon and Tea Tree Hand Sanitizer..........38
Oregano and Aloe Hand Sanitizer...................39
Tea Tree and Eucalyptus Hand Sanitizer.........40
Lemon Essential Oil Gel.................................40
Aloe Vera Gel Disinfectant..............................41
Myrtle and Aloe Essential Oil Gel....................41
Carrageenan Hand Sanitizer..........................42
Carrageenan and Sandal Hand Sanitizer.........43
Simple Disinfectant Recipe.............................44
Vitamin E and Rosemary Disinfectant Recipe. .44
Tea Tree Oil Disinfectant Recipe.....................45
Orange and Aloe Vera Disinfector...................46
Orange and Lemon Hand Disinfector..............46
Lavender Oil Disinfectant................................47
Vitamin E and Tea Tree Oil Disinfectant Recipe 47
Coconut Oil Hand Disinfector..........................48

Thyme and Aloe Disinfectant..........................48
Clove and Tea Tree Oil Disinfectant.................49
Cinnamon, Eucalyptus Hand Disinfector..........50
Cinnamon Disinfectant Spray.........................50
Oregano and Aloe Disinfectant.......................51
Tea Tree Oil Hand Disinfector........................52
Four Ingredients Hand Sanitizer......................52
Batch Hand Sanitizer......................................53
Four Ingredient Hand Sanitizer II....................55
Original Hand Sanitizer..................................55
Hand Sanitizer with Vitamin E........................56
DIY Hand Sanitizer..56
Liquid Soap...57

Chapter 6 Sanitizer Wipes.....................59
Homemade Sanitizer Wipes............................59
Antibacterial Wipes..60
Sanitizer Wipes №1..61
Sanitizer Wipes №2..63
Sterilizer Wipes..65

Conclusion...67

Introduction

If you are looking for a better way to keep yourself and your family deadly coronavirus infection-free, then you have landed in the right place. Coronavirus or Covid-19 is a contagious virus, and it is spreading rapidly. One of the main ways coronavirus spreads is by touching an infected object or surface with your hands. Using water and soap can kill the virus, but they are not readily available everywhere. You need alcohol-based hand sanitizers to instantly disinfectant your hands and avoid the risk of infections.

The same goes for the face masks. Although WHO and CDC assure us that healthy people do not need face masks and only infected people, caregivers and health workers need them. However, during this deadly pandemic, you want to take every measure to calm your nerves and keep you and your family safe. So, it is understandable that you might be looking for face masks. The bad news is, most of the grocery stores are out of face masks or selling them at an inflated price. Additionally, during this lockdown period, it not wise to go out in public places such as grocery stores to buy face masks and put yourself in danger. In this book, you will find various methods to make face masks with easily accessible resources.

If you happen to be one of those who couldn't find a face mask, a disinfectant, hand sanitizer or wipes for personal use, then there is no reason for you to panic. This comprehensive coronavirus survival book will show you how to make your own hand sanitizers, disinfectants, wipes, and face masks with materials you already have at home or that you can easily get in your local drugstore. Why worry about buying hand sanitizers and face masks when you can make your own at home? During this coronavirus pandemic, there is a scarcity of alcohol-based sanitizer and face masks. Making your own sanitizer and face masks at home will save you money and will protect you from this infectious Covid-19 virus.

This guide will allow you to easily make your own homemade face masks, wipes, disinfectants, and hand sanitizers, which are highly effective against infectious viruses and bacteria. If you find yourself in need of face masks, wipes, disinfectants, and hand sanitizers, then with the help of this book, you can make your own within minutes with just a few simple ingredients and steps. This book walks you through the process of making your own wipes, face masks, and sanitizers to keep yourself and your family safe. Additionally, you may need to avoid store-bought disinfectants, sanitizers, and wipes due to skin reactions and allergies.

Most store-bought sanitizers ae known to have a pungent and unpleasant scent. This book contains easy and straightforward homemade hand sanitizers and disinfectants that use natural and accessible ingredients that will enable you to make your personalized sanitizers for your skin type at home. Don't wait anymore, scroll up and hit the Buy Now button immediately to start preparing your wipes, sanitizers, disinfectants, and face masks. Get your copy now!

Chapter 1 Face Masks

As the coronavirus has become a pandemic, everyone is trying to buy masks and wear them. N95 and disposable face masks are useful because they block large particles from entering your mouth. Especially, N95 masks are tight-fitting and more effective against airborne diseases. Both of these masks are useful for protecting you from a viral infection such as Covid-19.

However, US health experts and doctors are saying that the American public should not purchase face masks and wear them to protect themselves from Covid-19. They are recommending that only infected people should wear masks to prevent infecting others. Along with US health officials, CDC (Centers for Disease Control and Prevention) also recommend that people do not use face masks to avoid Covid-19 infection. The organization is saying that only people who are showing the coronavirus symptoms should wear masks.

However, people are not listening. They are buying face masks, and both N95 and disposable masks have sold out in many parts of the US and Europe. Currently, the face masks are selling quickly on Walmart or Amazon.com at a higher price.

A better way to protect yourself

A better way to protect yourself is to wash your hands regularly, rather than wearing masks. You need to follow basic hygiene tips:

1. Wash your hands with soap and water for at least 20 seconds
2. Or use an alcohol-based hand sanitizer to disinfect your hands.
3. Do not touch your face (eyes, nose, and mouth) with unclean hands. If you need to cough or sneeze, then cover your mouth with your elbow.
4. Stay home when you are sick.
5. Disinfect regularly touched surfaces often.

Chapter 2 Different Types of Face masks and Who Needs them During the Coronavirus Pandemic

All of the masks, explained

MASK	USE	DESCRIPTION	USUAL COST	WHO NEEDS FOR COVID-19
Surgical mask (disposable)	Surgeons (mainly, so they don't get germs on their patients)	Can help protect wearers from getting others sick through their spit. Doesn't protect healthy people from acquiring an illness, and a loose fit leaves room for error.	$0.25	Sick people (to avoid infecting others), and caretakers
N95 respirator (disposable)	Working with dust, mold, or medical/environmental emergencies. Only protects against particles, not gases or vapors.	Can help protect healthcare workers from germs by blocking out at least 95% of small airborne particles — if worn correctly.	$2–$4	Healthcare workers
P100 respirator/ gas mask (reusable)	Painting/ woodworking, exposure to lead, asbestos, solvents and chemicals.	Protects manual laborers from exposure to lead, asbestos, solvents, and other dangerous chemicals on the job.	$25–$50	No one
Full face respirator/ Powered air-purifying respirator (reusable)	Painting or scenarios where a person needs protection from gases and vapors. Protects the eyes.	Protects people from gases and vapors. Can be a better fit for people with breathing problems or robust facial hair.	Prices vary. Start around $115 for basic models.	Could be for people who have a hard time breathing in a regular mask, as some are powered with an air supply.
Self-contained breathing apparatus (reusable)	Firefighters	Protects people like firefighters who need clean air in dangerously polluted situations.	$2,500–$4,000	No one

Sources: JAMA, FDA, OSHA, CDC

Face masks:

Since the coronavirus outbreak, face masks are in high demand. Don't panic during this coronavirus pandemic. According to the CDC, only sick people, caregivers, and healthcare workers need to wear masks. Wearing masks will help prevent coronavirus/Covid-19 droplets from spreading. Healthy people do not need face masks.

All masks are not the same. Face masks such as N95 are ideal for people who are sick with coronavirus. The mask also helps health workers to stay safe when they treat coronavirus infected people. Expensive full-face masks/respirators are needed by healthcare professionals who can't wear an N95 mask or people who have breathing problems in regular masks.

Chapter 3 Make Face Masks at Home

Safety Face Mask Recipe № 1

Tools:

- o   Kitchen towel
- o   A few rubber-bands

Method:

1. Take 2 or 3 layers of kitchen towels from the roll.
2. Now you need to fold it, horizontally, half-inch each time on either side.
3. So, fold once, ½ inch on one side, then fold ½ inch on the other side.
4. Continue until you finish folding.
5. Then use rubber bands to tie a knot on both edges of the folded paper towel. Or you can use a stapler to secure each end.
6. Now open up the mask and place it over your nose.
7. Use the rubber bands to secure the face mask on your face. (use the

rubber bands to attach the mask to your ears).

Safety Face Mask Recipe № 2

Tools:

- One shopping bag made from cloth or plastic
- A pair of scissors
- Several needlepoint pins
- Needle and thread
- Hot glue gun
- Elastic bands or long rubber bands

Method:

1. First, cut a piece of a cloth shopping bag with scissors. It should be 18cms to 20cms.
2. Then fold ½ inch (from the 18cms end) and insert 2 needlepoint pins on both ends to secure the fold.
3. Then again fold and secure with needlepoint pins
4. Continue until you finish folding.
5. Then sew both ends with needle and thread and remove the pins.

6. Also, you can use a hot glue gun to secure then ends even more.
7. Sew 2 elastic bands on both ends of the mask.
8. Now you are ready to use the mask!

Reversible and Washable Face Mask Recipe №3

Tools:

- A pair of scissors
- A disposable mask
- Needle and thread
- 2 types of fabrics
- Lampin (a cloth diaper) or burp cloth
- Elastic

Method:

1. First, fold the mask (sideways) and then stretch it. Then fold the cloth.
2. Place the folded face mask on the cloth and mark the measurement.
3. Remember to measure the cloth about ½ inch bigger than the size of the face mask.

4. Then cut the cloth, and you will get 2 pieces of clothes that are the same size as a folded face mask.
5. Do the same with the other fabric.
6. Cut the lampin or burp cloth according to the cut fabric parts.
7. Then use needle and thread to attach the burp to one of the cut cloth parts.
8. Then cover the burp side with the other cut part of the cloth and sew to attach.
9. Stitch the elastic bands on both sides, and your face mask is ready to use.

Homemade DIY N95 Type Face Mask Recipe №4

Tools:

- A MERV 13 filter
- A pair of scissors
- A glue gun
- A pair of leggings or a t-shirt
- Rubber bands
- A maxi pad **
- Tinfoil

Method:

1. First, remove the cardboard strips from the outer layer of the filter.
2. Now measure out 6 inches by 9 inches and cut it with a pair of scissors
3. Now pull back the net type material from the cut filter part.
4. Cut about 7 inches from one leg of the leggings or one t-shirt sleeve. Also cut a 1-inch strip (about 10 inches long). Now open the fold.
5. The MERV filter material already has layers that you can use as a measurement to fold.
6. Now tie each filter end with rubber bands. And then open the filter from the middle a bit.
7. Now open the maxi pad and remove the stick back. Now fold the maxi pad in half and cut, so it fits on the filter material.
8. Now place drops of hot glue on the edges of the filter material and fold the cut leggings part, so they are attached to the filter material.

9. Fold 12-inches of tinfoil and secure it on the top part of your mask with glue.
10. Cut a hole on each edge of your mask and use that 1-inch strip to make a sling.
11. Place it over your mouth, covering your nose, and bind the strip behind your head to make it secure.

Medical Mask at Home

Tools:

- Cotton wool
- Gauze
- Scissors
- Needle and thread
- Elastic

Method:

1. Cut four pieces of gauze (15x25 centimeters)
2. Now cut four strips of 5x30 centimeters from gauze.

3. Then press the four strips with an iron to make them smooth. You will use them as ribbons for your mask.
4. Now place the ribbons on the mask and bind them in the middle, just like the picture.
5. Top with the remaining layers of gauze and stitch along the perimeter.
6. Unscrew the mask, and your mask is ready.

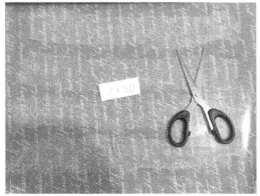

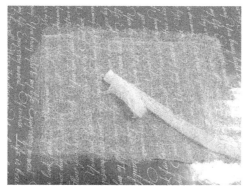

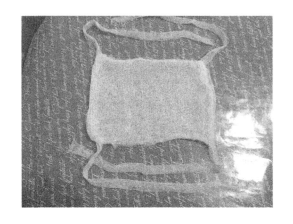

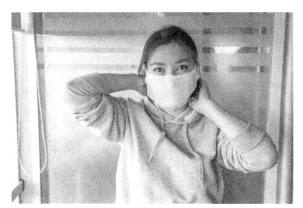

Chapter 4 WHO and CDC Hand Washing Recommendations

CDC recommends that you wash your hands:

1. Before, during, and after you finish preparing your food
2. Before eating
3. Before and after caring for a sick person
4. Before and after nursing a wound or cut
5. After using the toilet
6. After changing diapers
7. After coughing, sneezing or blowing your nose
8. After touching animal feed, an animal or animal waste
9. After caring or feeding a pet
10. After touching garbage

5 steps to wash your hands:

1. Wet your hands with warm or cold, clean running water. Turn off the tap then apply soap.
2. Rub well to cover your hands with soap, lather between your fingers, backs of your hands, and under your nails.
3. Scrub your hands for a minimum of 20 seconds.
4. Rinse your hands.
5. Air dry your hands or use a clean towel.

Using hand sanitizers:

Using soap and water to clean your hands is the best way to protect yourself from coronavirus. You can use hand sanitizers if soap and water are not available. Make sure that the hand sanitizer is alcohol-based and contains at least 60% alcohol. Check the product level to know how much alcohol it contains.

Sanitizers reduce the number of germs on your hands, but:

- Sanitizers/disinfectants/ do not kill all types of germs

- If your hands are visibly greasy or dirty, then hand sanitizers won't be that effective
- Hand disinfectants/ sanitizers might not remove harmful chemicals such as heavy metals and pesticides.

How to use hand sanitizer:

- Read the label to learn the right amount to use.
- Then apply the product to the palm of one of your hands.
- Rub your hands together.
- Rub the hand sanitizer/disinfectant all over your hands. Cover everything, just like the previous handwashing technique but without the water. Rub your hands until they are dry, about 20 seconds.

Chapter 5 Homemade Hand Sanitizer Recipes

Basic Hand Sanitizer Recipe

Ingredients:

- o 1 2/3 cups isopropyl alcohol
- o 2 tbsps. glycerol
- o 1 tbsp. of hydrogen peroxide
- o ¼ cup of distilled or boiled, cool water

Method:

1. Add everything in a clean bowl.
2. Mix with a whisk.
3. Pour into a bottle with a dispenser pump and use.

Aloe Vera Hand Sanitizer

Ingredients:

- o ½ cup isopropyl alcohol

- ¼ cup aloe vera juice
- 10 drops cinnamon essential oil
- 10 drops orange essential oil
- 1 tbsp. of your favorite lotion

Method:

1. Add everything in a bowl.
2. Whisk with a whisk.
3. Pour into a bottle with a dispenser pump and use.

Rose Hand Sanitizer

Ingredients:

- ½ cup isopropyl alcohol
- ¼ cup EverClear (find it in alcohol shops)
- 10 drops rosemary essential oil
- 10 drops rose essential oil

Method:

1. Add everything in a bowl.

2. Mix a whisk.
3. Pour into a bottle with a dispenser pump and use.

Chamomile Hand Sanitizer

Ingredients:

- ½ cup isopropyl alcohol
- ¼ cup aloe vera juice
- 15 drops of Roman Chamomile essential oil

Method:

1. Add everything in a clean bowl.
2. Mix with a whisk.
3. Pour into a bottle with a dispenser pump and use.

Aloe Vera, and Tea Tree Hand Sanitizer

Ingredients:

- 1 cup of 91% isopropyl alcohol
- ½ cup of aloe vera gel

- 15 drops of tea tree oil

Method:

1. Add everything in a clean bowl.
2. Whisk to mix.
3. Pour into a clean bottle with a pouring spout.
4. Use.

Lemon and Lavender Hand Sanitizer

Ingredients:

- 40g distilled water
- 2g carrageenan
- 10g glycerin
- 45g Food-grade alcohol
- 8 drops of tea tree essential oil
- 10 drops of lemon essential oil
- 10 drops of lavender essential oil

Method:

1. Put water + carrageenan into a cup.
2. Mix with a tablespoon until you make a gel. Then let stand for 10 minutes.
3. Put food-grade alcohol + glycerin + essential oils into another cup
4. Mix with a spoon.
5. Use a hand blender with the carrageen gel (resulting from steps 1 + 2) adding the alcoholic solution (resulting from steps 3 + 4).
6. Put the liquid gel into a dispenser.
7. Use.

Basic Hand Sanitizer Recipe

Ingredients:

- 3 parts isopropyl alcohol (rubbing alcohol)
- 1-part aloe vera gel

Method:

1. Mix with a whisk, pour in a bottle, and use.

Aloe Vera and Grapefruit Hand Sanitizer

Ingredients:

- 1/3 cup aloe vera gel
- 2/3 cup isopropyl alcohol
- 8 drops of peppermint oil
- 8 drops of grapefruit oil

Method:

1. Mix everything with a whisk.
2. Pour in a bottle and use it.

Soothing Lavender Hand Sanitizer

Ingredients:

- 1 cup EverClear (from liquor store)
- ½ cup aloe vera gel
- 10 drops of lavender oil

Method:

1. Mix with a whisk, pour in a bottle, and use.

Aloe Vera and Lavender Hand Sanitizer

Ingredients:

- o 10 drops of lavender oil
- o 6 drops of lemongrass oil
- o 25 drops of tea tree oil
- o 1-ounce of aloe vera gel
- o 2 ounces of isopropyl alcohol
- o 1 tsp. of vitamin E oil

Method:

1. Mix everything with a whisk.
2. Pour into a bottle with a dispenser pump and use.

Tea Tree Hand Sanitizer

Ingredients:

- o ¼ cup aloe vera gel

- ½ tsp. glycerin
- 2/3 cup isopropyl alcohol
- 20 drops of tea tree oil
- 20 drops of peppermint oil

Method:
1. Mix everything with a whisk.
2. Pour in a bottle.
3. Use.

Aloe and Tea Tree Hand Sanitizer
Ingredients:
- 3 parts isopropyl alcohol
- 1-part aloe vera gel
- 30 drops of tea tree oil

Method:
1. Mix everything with a whisk.
2. Pour in a bottle.
3. Use.

Clove and Lavender Hand Sanitizer

Ingredients:

- 2/3 cup isopropyl
- ½ cup aloe vera gel
- 4 drops of orange oil
- 4 drops of cinnamon oil
- 2 drops of clove oil
- 2 drops of lavender oil

Method:

1. Mix everything with a whisk.
2. Pour in a bottle and use it.

Vitamin E and Tea Tree Oil Hand Sanitizer

Ingredients:

- ½ cup isopropyl alcohol
- ¼ cup aloe vera gel
- 10 drops of tea tree oil
- ½ tsp. vegetable glycerin

- 1 tsp. colloidal silver
- 5 drops of vitamin E oil
- 10 drops of lemon oil

Method:

1. Mix everything with a whisk.
2. Pour in a bottle and use it.

Aloe and Eucalyptus Hand Sanitizer

Ingredients:

- ½ cup isopropyl alcohol
- ¼ cup aloe vera juice
- 10 drops of eucalyptus oil
- 10 drops of rosemary oil
- 1 tbsp. of vegetable glycerin

Method:

1. Mix everything with a whisk.
2. Pour in a bottle and use it.

Aloe Vera Hand Sanitizer

Ingredients:

- ¾ cup isopropyl alcohol
- ¼ cup aloe vera gel
- 10 drops of orange oil
- 1 tbsp. of your favorite lotion

Method:

1. Mix everything with a whisk.
2. Pour in a bottle and use it.

Roman Chamomile and Aloe Vera Hand Sanitizer

Ingredients:

- ¾ cup isopropyl alcohol
- ¼ cup aloe vera gel
- 10 drops of Roman chamomile oil

Method:

1. Mix everything with a whisk.

2. Pour in a bottle and use it.

Basic Hand Sanitizer

Ingredients:

- ¾ cup of isopropyl or rubbing alcohol (99%)
- ¼ cup of aloe vera gel
- 10 drops of essential oil of your choice

Method:

1. Add everything in a bowl.
2. Mix with a whisk until mixed well.
3. Pour in a bottle and use it.

Hand Sanitizer Recipe

Ingredient:

- 4.8 oz. 96% ethyl alcohol
- 0.3 oz. .3% hydrogen peroxide
- 0.15 oz. glycerin
- 0.8 distilled and sterilized water

Method:

1. Mix with a whisk and pour in a bottle.
2. Let is rest for 72 hours and use it.

Vinegar Disinfectant
Ingredients:

- o 50 ml of vinegar
- o 50 ml of distilled water
- o 2 ml tea tree essential tea oil

Method:

1. Mix vinegar, water, and tea tree essential oil.
2. Add in the bottle and shake well.
3. Use.

Lavender Disinfectant
Ingredients:

- o 100 ml aloe vera gel

- 20 drops of natural tea tree essential oil
- 10 drops of natural essential oil of lavender

Method:

1. Mix everything and use it.

Cinnamon and Tea Tree Hand Sanitizer

Ingredients:

- 25ml aloe vera gel
- 100ml food grade alcohol
- 10 drops of cinnamon essential oil
- 10 drops of tea tree essential oil
- 30ml distilled water

Method:

1. Mix aloe vera gel, glycerin, and food-grade alcohol in a bowl.
2. Add cinnamon and tea tree essential oils.

3. Mix well and add water.
4. Store and use when needed.

Oregano and Aloe Hand Sanitizer

Ingredients:

- 40ml distilled water
- 40ml aloe gel
- 200ml food grade alcohol
- 1.5 g of vegetable glycerin
- 30 drops of tea tree essential oil
- 15 drops of oregano essential oil

Method:

1. Pour the distilled water into a glass.
2. Add the aloe gel and mix.
3. Pour the alcohol in another glass.
4. Add the glycerin and the essential oils and mix carefully.
5. Add the alcohol solution to the gel and slowly stir.

6. Store in a clean bottle and use as required.

Tea Tree and Eucalyptus Hand Sanitizer

Ingredients:

- 300ml food grade alcohol
- 15 drops essential tea tree oil
- 30 drops eucalyptus essential oil
- 100 ml aloe vera gel

Method:

1. Mix the oils together and add food-grade alcohol.
2. Add the aloe vera and pour the mix into a bottle.
3. Shake before use.

Lemon Essential Oil Gel

Ingredients:

- 30ml aloe vera gel
- 7 drops of cinnamon essential oil
- 8 drops of lemon essential oil

- o 50ml distilled water

Method:

1. Use 30 ml aloe vera as a base.
2. Add 15 drops of cinnamon and lemon essential oils
3. Dilute everything with 50ml of distilled water and mix well.
4. Shake and use.

Aloe Vera Gel Disinfectant

Ingredients:

- o 50 ml aloe vera gel
- o 8 drops of tea tree essential oil
- o 5 drops of Mandarin essential oil

Method:

1. Mix the elements and pour them into a container with a dispenser.
2. Shake and use.

Myrtle and Aloe Essential Oil Gel

Ingredients:

- 50ml aloe vera gel
- 50ml food grade alcohol
- 7 drops of myrtle essential oil

Method:

1. Mix everything well.
2. Store in a glass bottle.

Carrageenan Hand Sanitizer

Ingredients:

- 15ml carrageenan
- 50ml of distilled water
- 10g of vegetable glycerin
- 200 ml of food-grade alcohol
- 7 drops of scotch pine essential oil

Method:

1. Pour the water into a glass and add the carrageenan

2. Mix and let the solution rest until it has formed a gel.

3. In another glass pour, the food-grade alcohol. Add the glycerin and add the essential oil. Mix gently.

4. Add the alcohol solution to the gel and stir slowly.

5. Transfer to clean bottle

6. Use.

Carrageenan and Sandal Hand Sanitizer

Ingredients:

- 15 ml carrageenan
- 50 ml distilled water
- 10 g of vegetable glycerin
- 200 ml of food-grade alcohol
- 8 drops of sandalwood essential oil

Method:

1. Pour the water into a glass and add the carrageenan.
2. Stir well and let the solution rest until it has formed a gel.
3. In a bowl, pour the alcohol. Add the glycerin and the essential oils. Mix gently.
4. Add the alcohol solution to the gel and mix slowly.
5. Store in a bottle.

Simple Disinfectant Recipe

Ingredients:

- 4 tbsp. of rubbing alcohol
- 2 tbsp. of glycerin
- 2 drops of peppermint essential oil

Method:

1. Add the ingredients in a bowl and mix with a whisk to mix.

2. Use a funnel to pour the liquid into a bottle with a dispenser or a spray bottle.

Vitamin E and Rosemary Disinfectant Recipe

Ingredients:

- Alcohol
- Almond oil
- 5 drops of rosemary essential oil
- 5 drops of vitamin E

Method:

1. Take alcohol and almond oil in the ratio of 2:1 for a liquid solution.
2. For gel – 1:1.
3. Add vitamin E and rosemary oil. Whisk to mix and pour it into a bottle with a dispenser.

Tea Tree Oil Disinfectant Recipe

Ingredients:

- 5 / 10 drops of lavender essential oil

- 1 tbsp. of alcohol
- 30 drops of tea tree oil
- 25 drops of a solution of vitamin E
- 7.9 ounces of aloe vera gel

Method:

1. Mix everything and pour it into a plastic bottle with a dispenser.
2. Use.

Orange and Aloe Vera Disinfector

Ingredients:

- 1 tbsp. of aloe vera gel
- 3.4 ounces of distilled water
- 10 drops of clove and eucalyptus essential oil
- 20 drops of orange essential oil for aroma

Method:

1. Mix everything in a bowl. Pour into a bottle and use it.

Orange and Lemon Hand Disinfector

Ingredients:

- 3.4 ounces of hamamelis (also known as witch hazel) extract
- 2 tsps. Of liquid coconut oil or vitamin E oil
- 5 drops of essential oils of orange, lemon balm, rosemary and cinnamon
- 10 drops of lemon essential oil

Method:

1. Mix everything in a bowl with a whisk.
2. Pour into a bottle with a dispenser pump and use.

Lavender Oil Disinfectant

Ingredients:

- 3.4 ounces of hamamelis (also known as witch hazel) extract
- 10 drops of lavender oil

Method:

1. Add lavender oil to the hamamelis solution and shake it.
2. Use.

Vitamin E and Tea Tree Oil Disinfectant Recipe

Ingredients:

- 3 tbsps. of aloe gel
- 10 drops of tea tree oil
- 5 drops peach seed oil
- 5 drops of vitamin E
- 5 drops each of lavender and bergamot essential oils

Method:

1. Add tea tree oil in aloe gel. Mix well.
2. Add peach seed oil and vitamin E. Mix again.
3. Add lavender and bergamot essential oils and mix again.

4. Pour into a bottle and shake it.

Coconut Oil Hand Disinfector
Ingredients:

- o   1.5 tbsps. of alcohol
- o   3.4 ounces of distilled water
- o   1 tsp. liquid coconut oil
- o   5 drops of cinnamon essential oil

Method:

1. Mix thoroughly all the ingredients together and pour the mixture into a bottle.

Thyme and Aloe Disinfectant
Ingredients:

- o   8 tbsps. aloe vera gel
- o   15 drops of tea tree oil
- o   10 drops of lavender oil
- o   5 drops of thyme essential oil

Method:

1. Mix all the ingredients and put it in a bottle with the dispenser.

Clove and Tea Tree Oil Disinfectant

Ingredients:

- 8 tbsps. aloe vera gel
- 5 tbsps. of alcohol
- 2 drops of tea tree oil
- 2 drops of clove oil

Method:

1. Mix everything in a bottle. Shake well.
2. Use.

Cinnamon, Eucalyptus Hand Disinfector

Ingredients:

- 5 tbsps. of hamamelis (also known as witch hazel)
- 12 tbsps. of pure aloe vera gel

- 5 drops of clove essential oil
- 4 drops of lime essential oil
- 3 drops of cinnamon essential oil
- 2 drops of eucalyptus essential oil
- 1 drop of rosemary essential oil
- 5 drops of vitamin E oil

Method:

1. Mix hamamelis and aloe vera, add essential oils and vitamin E, and mix well. Pour the liquid into a bottle.
2. Use.

Cinnamon Disinfectant Spray

Ingredients:

- 1 tbsp. of alcohol
- 4 tbsps. of aloe vera gel
- Distilled water
- ½ tsp. of vegetable glycerin
- 10 drops of cinnamon essential oil

- o 10 drops of tea tree essential oil
- o 4 drops of vanilla essential oil

Method:

1. Mix aloe vera gel, glycerin, and alcohol. Add oil and mix well. Add as much distilled water as needed for the desired consistency and mix again.
2. Put the mixture into the spray dispenser.

Oregano and Aloe Disinfectant
Ingredients:

- o 10 tbsps. plus 2 tsps. of alcohol
- o 5 tbsps. plus 1 tsp. of aloe vera gel
- o 8 to 10 drops of essential oregano oil

Method:

1. Mix all the ingredients and then pour the product into the bottle.

Tea Tree Oil Hand Disinfector

Ingredients:

- 4 tbsps. of aloe gel
- 1 tbsp. of glycerin
- 4 tbsps. of hamamelis (also known as witch hazel)
- 1 tbsp. of vinegar
- 8 /10 drops of tea tree oil

Method:

1. Mix all the ingredients.
2. Pour it into a container.
3. Shake well and use it.

Four Ingredients Hand Sanitizer

Ingredients:

- 833 ml food-grade alcohol
- 3 tbsps. 3% hydrogen peroxide
- 15 ml glycerin

- o Distilled water as needed to reach 1 liter

Method:

1. Pour the alcohol into a bowl.
2. Add hydrogen peroxide and mix.
3. Add 15 mls of glycerin and mix it again.
4. Pour distilled water.
5. Mix and pour in a bottle.
6. Use.

Batch Hand Sanitizer

This recipe will make about 2.5 gallons worth of handwash

Ingredients:

- o Ethanol 96% or isopropyl alcohol, 99.8%: 2.2 gallons of ethanol or 2 gallons of isopropyl alcohol.
- o Hydrogen peroxide 3%: 1 ¾ cups
- o Glycerol 98%: 0.6 cups

- o   Sterile distilled or boiled cold water

Tools:

- o   2.6 gallon (plastic bottle) to 13.2 gallons (plastic tank)
- o   Wooden, plastic, or metal paddles for mixing
- o   Measuring cylinders and measuring jugs
- o   An alcoholometer
- o   Plastic or metal funnel

(the recipes can be prepared in 10-liter glass or plastic bottles)

Method:

1. The actual materials you will need to mix the ingredients depends on how much you want to make.
2. Pour in the alcohol, then hydrogen peroxide, glycerol, and cover to seal.
3. Mix the solution by shaking gently or by using a paddle.

4. Remember, set aside this solution for 72 hours before use.

5. Important: place the solution in quarantine for 72 hours before use.

Four Ingredient Hand Sanitizer II
Ingredients:

- 1 cup of 99% isopropyl alcohol
- 1 tbsp. of 3% hydrogen peroxide
- 1 tsp. of 98% glycerin
- ¼ cup, 1 tbsp. and 1 tsp. of sterile distilled or boiled cold water

Method:

1. Add everything in a clean bowl. Whisk to mix.
2. Pour in a clean bottle and use it.

Original Hand Sanitizer
Ingredients:

- 28 ounces of ethyl alcohol

- 1.40 ounces of a 3% hydrogen peroxide
- 1 tbsp. of glycerin
- ½ cup Distilled water

Method:

1. Mix everything in a clean bowl with a whisk.
2. Pour into a clean bottle with a dispenser pump.
3. Use.

Hand Sanitizer with Vitamin E
Ingredients:

- ½ cup aloe vera juice
- ¼ cup vodka
- 10 drops of anti-bacterial essential oils: clove, tea tree, cinnamon, thyme, or orange
- 1 tbsp. organic lavender lotion
- 1 tbsp. vegetable glycerin

Method:

1. Add everything in a blender and blend well.
2. Pour into a bottle and use it.
3. Store away from sunlight.

DIY Hand Sanitizer

Ingredients:

- 1 cup 99% isopropyl alcohol
- 1 tbsp. 3% hydrogen peroxide
- 1 tsp. 90% glycerin
- Enough sterile or boiled, cold water to bring the total mixture to 1 1/3 cups

Method:

1. Mix everything in a bowl with a whisk.
2. Store in a bottle.

Remember using isopropyl alcohol diluted beyond 91% will result in a weaker hand sanitizer that doesn't meet the CDC's 60% benchmark.

We have discussed a lot of hand sanitizer recipes. Here is one recipe to make your own soap.

Liquid Soap

Ingredients:

- Distilled or boiled, cool water
- Castile soap
- Almond oil
- Vegetable glycerin
- Essential oils of your choice
- Glass hand pump

Method:

1. Add soap into the pump container (fill it about ¼ full).
2. Now add 2 tbsps. of almond oil
3. 1 tbsp. of glycerin
4. 15 drops of lavender, tea tree 10 drops, cedarwood atlas 10 drops.
5. Fill to the top with water.

6. Shake and use.

Chapter 6 Sanitizer Wipes

Homemade Sanitizer Wipes

Ingredients:

- 1 clean, old t-shirt (cut up to use them as wipes)
- Scissors
- A large jar
- 1 cup filtered or distilled water
- ½ cup of vinegar
- ¼ cup rubbing alcohol (70% alcohol concentration at least)
- 1 tsp. liquid castile soap
- 8 to 12 drops of essential oils from 2 of the following: lavender, tea tree, germ fighter, lemon, and any kind of citrus

Method:

1. Add all the liquid ingredients together in the jar and mix.

2. Add in wipes in the jar and allow them to absorb the liquid. Cover the jar and shake well.

3. The wipes should be fully damp but not sopping. Add a bit more water if needed.

4. Cover well and store in a cool, dry place.

Antibacterial Wipes

Ingredients:

- 1 ¼ cup isopropyl alcohol (70% and above)
- 1 tbsp. hydrogen peroxide
- 1 tsp. glycerin
- ¼ cup distilled water
- 30 paper towels cut in half
- Airtight container for storage

Method:

1. Mix the ingredients in a clean bowl with a whisk.

2. In a clean storage container, stack paper towels.

3. Pour the mixture over the paper towels.

4. Close the lid and shake well.

5. Make sure all the paper towels get soaked well.

6. Shake well before each use.

Sanitizer Wipes №1

Tools:

- 1-pound coffee canister with plastic lid
- Scissors
- Needle
- Spray paint
- 10 drops of essential oil
- 1 tsp. liquid dish soap
- ¼ tsp. rubbing alcohol
- ¼ cup of water

- ½ cup vinegar
- Sharp knife
- Paper towel roll

Method:

1. With a knife, cut the paper towels in half.
2. Squish them into the painted can.
3. Mix the water, alcohol, dish soap, few drops of essential oil, and vinegar in a bowl.
4. Gently pour the liquid over the paper towels.
5. Saturate them. Then gently remove the cardboard center and pull a paper towel from the center.
6. Cut a 1 ½ inch diameter circle in the center of the plastic lid.
7. Pass a bit of the paper towel through the hole and cover the can with the lid.
8. You can add a few drops of water into the canister to keep the wipes moist.
9. Use!

Sanitizer Wipes №2

Ingredient:

- 2 cups of warm water
- 1 cup of rubbing alcohol (at least 70% alcohol concentration)
- 1 tbsp. dish soap

Method:

1. Mix the ingredients well.
2. Add this blend to half a roll of paper towels in a Tupperware box.

Sterilizer Wipes
Tools:

- o   A paper towel roll
- o   A knife
- o   Bleach
- o   Water
- o   Container

Method:

1. Measure the paper towel and cut in half.
2. Mix ¼ cup splash less chlorine to 2 ¼ water
3. Remove cardboard core from the paper towel
4. Place the paper towel in the container.
5. Allow the mixture to absorb into the paper towel.
6. Use.

Here are other recipes without bleach

- o   ½ cup vinegar

- 1 cup of water
- 1 tsp. liquid dish soap
- 5 to 10 drops essential oil

Essential oil wipes

- ¼ cup of water
- 1 tsp. dish soap
- 1 cup rubbing alcohol
- 5 /10 drops of an essential oil blend

Mix and pour over paper towels.

Conclusion

Properly rubbing your hands with hand sanitizers is one of the best ways to avoid the coronavirus infection. Using soap and water is the best method of cleaning your hands, but they are not easily available in every place. You need to carry a hand sanitizer to protect your health. This book includes homemade hand sanitizers, disinfectants, wipes, and face mask making methods that any beginner can do. If you are unable to find a hand sanitizer in stores, then this book will make you feel calm and prepared.

Made in the USA
Monee, IL
05 April 2020